A Sight to Behold

Ann B. Rhodes

A Sight to Behold
Copyright © 2018 Ann B. Rhodes

All rights reserved. No part(s) of this book may be reproduced, distributed or transmitted in any form, or by any means, or stored in a database or retrieval systems without prior expressed written permission of the author of this book.

ISBN: 978-1-5356-1588-4

Dedication

This book is dedicated to my mother, Alma Rhodes, my supporter through anything that I set out to do, my two brothers, Bennie and Roy, my niece, Tianna, my nephew, Malcolm and a special friend who helped me come up with the title.

Contents

Section 1: Eternal Life
    My Final Resting Place 8
    I Wish You Were Not Dead 10
    Going Home 11
    A Great Woman 13

Section 2: Having the Holy Spirit
    Change 16
    Appreciating Life 17
    My Spiritual Plan 18
    My True Light 20
    The One Who Encourages 21
    Listen 22
    It Was a Calling 23
    Stepping Out on Faith 24
    Changes Through Life (Middle School Life) 25
    Surviving the Storm 27
    Experiencing a Breakthrough 28
    I Wish I Would Have Listened 29
    Church 31

Section 3: Relationships
    If I Could See You Face to Face 34
    Thinking I'm in Love 37
    It's Worth the Wait! 39
    As My Dreams Come True 41
    True Love 42
    May My Dream Come True 43
    How It Should Have Been 44
    What Is a Dad? 46
    For the Father I Never Had 47
    Dear Mama 48
    If Only You Were Here 49

Section 4: Holidays and Months
January 52
February 53
He Bore the Cross for Me 54
To My Mother, With Love 55
What Is a Mother? 56
My Mother's Love 57

Section 5: School Thoughts
It Was Here Today, But Gone Tomorrow 60
School Days 62
Life Choices 63
Testing Prayer 64
Graduation Wisdom 66
School Changes 67
Happy Birthday, Mr. Wearden! 68
Jaime Smith 69
Mrs. Williams 70
Mrs. Pflueger 71
Bennie Rhodes, Jr. (My Brother) 72
Mrs. Spradlin 73
A Teacher and Teaching 74
What Is a Teacher? 75

Section 6: Other Poems
Where I Go, Someone's There 78
It Was Just a Test 80
Stand by Me 81
What Is a Family? 82
Work Hard for Your Blessings 83
Faith Is my Belief 84
My Gift 85
The Saxophone 86
What Is Being Faithful? 87

About the Author 89

Section 1:
Eternal Life

My Final Resting Place

When Jesus brought the angels down from heaven,
I knew they were preparing me for my final resting place.
As I spoke to the people on my earthly home,
I knew I was about to win this race.

You see, God had already spoken to me
And told me it was time for my number to be called.
From the gates of heaven the angels were waiting for me
To walk proudly with my wings down the hall.

As the angels stood and looked
They whispered, "You have earned your angel wings with your actions from being a respectful soul,
We thank you for all of your peace, comfort, and praises that you would sing."

As this transition takes place,
I would like to say to my friends and family,
"God has shown me the colorful rainbow to follow the path to gold.
Therefore, there is no need to weep.
And shed a lot of tears over me.

Today is the day I am healed,
Because Jesus has released me to become free.
I have fought a good fight,
I have finished my course,
I have kept the faith (2 Timothy 4:7).

Now that I am at my final resting place
I am celebrating every day.
Because my Lord, my Savior, came down and saved me.

He knew my body and eyes were tired
So it was time for me to go.
God wanted my spirit to leave this old body
So now I can become whole.

I know that my earthly family and friends
Don't understand why I had to leave;
God still has a plan for me
To move on to bigger and better things.

Now that I am your guardian angel
And your guide along the way,
My spirit will always be with you
On the good days and the bad.

I may whisper something in your ear,
Or the wind may blow a certain way,
A bird may land on your windowsill;
It's a sign from me that everything is going to be okay.

Don't worry about me now;
Only pray that I will see you one day
And we can enjoy our heavenly home,
That is our final resting place.

I Wish You Were Not Dead

I wish you were not dead.
I have so much I have to say.
I could always talk to you
Because you gave me a sense of hope along the way.

Things are so different
Since you left this earthly place.
I'm having difficulty handling
These trials and tribulations without seeing your bright, smiling face.

I suddenly hear a sound,
"Click!" As the silver bars begin to close.
I feel like I'm trapped behind a wall
Sitting still now with no place to go.

In my time of adversity,
I knew you were a phone call away,
But now I must look up to heaven
And hope that you hear me pray.

I want your sweet, energetic spirit
To come back and walk with me.
Maybe you can help me with these decisions
So one day I shall be free.

These silver bars will be unlocked
So I can walk right path down the road
And appreciate my freedom with respect and honor to our country.

Going Home
(Dedicated to the late Eunice Ann Hardaway, 1933–2016)

Joy comes in the morning
As the angels begin to appear.
I see the bright light shining all around
As the end of my earthly home is coming near.

Several years ago, I began reading the Holy Bible every day;
I pray and talk to God to give me peace and comfort along the way.
On my earthly home I lost both of my legs and my life was completely different.
It made me close my eyes and reflect on the life that I have led.

There are many different things that I've done that I should have changed,
From the way I treated people to being a person full of lies.
The memory came back to me like a camera flash taking pictures during the night.
I kneel down and ask God for forgiveness for my selfish ways.

During my last moments on earth
I prayed and asked God for a complete healing
For the rest of the days I shall live.
God took away the pain so I could be physical healed, but
As I continued to pray, he guided me to the path where I could receive spiritual forgiveness.

When the Lord spoke to me
And told me it was time to come,
My heart was filled with excitement
Because entering in the kingdom where I received spiritual healing
is what I just won.

I was able to meet my family members who passed years ago.
Entering into the pearly gates is such a joyous occasion
For us to finally be back together again and erase all the hate.

As I have closed my eyes on earth
I open them in my eternal home where I am healed forever
And I have no more pain or suffering, only love.

I leave an only child and other family members on earth
Who don't understand the joy I am feeling.
God spoke to me and said, "Come to me, for complete healing."
To my only child, I am fully awake with God.
And I am at home watching you.
I am now the angel that is watching that will help you make it through.

A Great Woman
(Dedicated to Patti Teaver)

During my early twenties
I began a career filled with many sunny days and hurricanes,
But regardless of how many storms I encountered
There was one person who opened her ears.

On my tricky journey as a first-year teacher
My students were as different as the mysterious blue dusk and sunshine that was bright like a flashlight.
They had a grin on their face to walk into the counselor's office
And receive a reward for modeling exemplary behavior.
When students needed someone to talk to, Mrs. Teaver's voice was as soft as a flute saying,
"Everything is going to be just fine,"
Her heart spread with love for every student.
Her attentive watchful eyes and listening ears saved me in destructive tornadoes at parent meetings.

As the roller-coaster trip in teaching continues
My eyes sparkle as I smile at my former students walking down the hall.
Our close teamwork and day-by-day communication built solid groundwork for these students to travel on their thorny adventures into the next rank of learning.

Section 2:
Having the Holy Spirit

Change

In this journey of life
Many people who cross our paths come and go.
They have touched our lives and made an impact
And it's hard to wave your hand and say goodbye to them, as you know.

Change is a tool
That can burst things into pieces.
It can make you question
if you are traveling the right path.

Change is like ice;
It can melt to take on a new form.
You ask the question "Why?"
Why did things take a different turn?

Sometimes we wonder
Why God takes us a different way.
That's a question that will only be answered
If we drop down on your knees to pray.

God has our life planned out from the start date until the end
So do God's will and follow his directions and destination
So you will prevent committing a multitude of sins.

Appreciating Life

As the earth revolves, love spins brighter around the sun
To bring people closer together and unify peace like the gates of heaven.

As the sun rises in the morning,
It takes some hatred that's hot as the devil away
So the young generation has a chance to grow like the flowers outside
Or prosper like someone starting their own business.

As the bright orange sun sets at night above the house,
This sun takes away the sadness of sorrow like a grandmother weeping over a sick child
And encourages faith in the miracle of God.
That could change things along the way.

When a rainbow develops,
At the end of a pot of gold.
It represents all the of happiness of sunshine.

One can love and hear hummingbird's heartbeat
When a storm comes around and the fear of thunder scares you away,
It makes you appreciate the path called life
And how blessed it is to live each day.

My Spiritual Plan

As I wake up in the morning,
I drop down on my knees to pray.
I praise the Lord
For giving me another day.

Several people have often asked me in a soft whisper,
"What direction would you like to go in life?"
I reply in a strong, stern voice,
"I will let the Lord decide my sacrifice."

As an elementary school student,
I was as quiet as a mouse,
But as middle school student,
I lifted my voice so it could echo through the mountains.

As a high school student,
I was quiet and reserved,
I was always somewhere praying,
And waiting on guidance from the Lord.

When I graduate from high school in May,
To my teachers, administrators, and fellow peers,
If you don't remember anything,
Just remember that I said
"I walk by my faith and my belief in God.
It is stronger than a grain of a mustard seed.
The Lord is my Shepherd, I shall not want."

God has a plan in everybody's life,
Regardless if it's joy or sadness
The Lord leads me and guides me on my way through.
And always remember
I am following God's plan
And what he tells me to do.

Times can get rough like a rock,
But as an angel reaches the sky
She gives you a shield of protection
Wherever your trouble may lie.

My True Light
(In memory of Sue Ann Tyson)

She was a butterfly
Who spread sunshine and happiness
To all of the boys and girls.
Her calm voice was greater than a whisper to speak words of encouragement to them.

She was a fierce boxer
Who fought any predators who surprised her on her long, treacherous journey.
But no matter how rough things were,
She always would see that shining light at the end the tunnel.

She got her boxing gloves to help her fight any battle
While she filled her heart with ounces of hope and belief.
Her smiles were filled with happiness
Because she was receiving all of the peace that was needed.

She is the feather that I found in my path
That gave me strength greater than any food.
She was the flashlight that shined the light which guided me through any battle or war in education I had to face.
She was a soldier who taught everyone to put up a good fight.

But most of all she was a set of footprints
Who will leave an impression on all of our lives.
She was a true hero who has left footprints in our hearts.
(She was a guide who help me establish the foundation at the beginning of my career. She always had a positive word about any challenge in the classroom.)

The One Who Encourages

I'm your guardian angel from heaven
Whose spirit is watching from above.
I'm now a bird who's spread my wings
To send this special song with a message of love.

The year is 2018
And you've made it down a long, treacherous path.
These four years have been a journey
But you made it through the grapes of wrath.

Your head is held high looking toward the mountain
Because of the teaching from when you were young.
Now you are about to travel into the world,
And that song of love you will always be singing.

As you graduate in the month of May,
Stand tall and have no fears of this world.
Just remember all those life lessons and how to cope.
Keep God first and your guardian angel will always give you hope.

Listen

Life can get as tough as nails,
And hit you like a ton of bricks.
A coat of protection can come around
Wherever your trouble may lie.

This shield will protect you
From Satan and the fire that is straight ahead.
Everywhere you go,
Your angel will be your shining light,
Even through the difficult times,
So your happiness will be bright.

The devil can torch your finances
And make you lose everything.
Your true friends will stick by your side,
While others will leave because they tried to play you.

Stay strong in the Lord,
For he will reveal the path you have to take
Patience is a virtue.
Stand beside God and he will get you through any storm.

It Was a Calling

As God walks with you in the path of your life,
You never know the journeys or obstacles you will have to face,
But as long as you hang on to God's unchanging hand,
He'll stand beside you to run the race.

Sometimes God can touch you
And allow you to discover that special talent that you have received.
You have to pray and ask God for guidance
Because the devil will try to take you through the wrath.

As I dropped down on my knees to pray
A bright light appeared before my eyes.
There stood an angel with her wings wide open, saying,
"God has given you a gift, why are you not using it?"

God has given me a talent
But it was my choice not to use,
Yet when it's a gift from God,
Then you will always be led on what to do.

When the Holy Spirit
Lays hands on you and shows you the way to go,
Smile and look up to the heavens.
Remember it's a calling by the grace of God;
It's not what your heart led you to do.

Stepping Out on Faith

I want your sweet, energetic spirit
To stand and walk with me.
Maybe you can help me with these decisions
So one day I shall be free.

Sometimes I feel like
God is sending me a vivid message
If I continue to the path of darkness,
A bolt of lightning can struck my way.

If I go down the path of a shining light
But, God, you have planted the seed,
So in my mind I must obey.

The seed has grown over a course of months
Where it's sprouted into a beautiful plant
But I drop down on my knees to pray again
Because of the pain and throbbing heartache.

My heart is pounding with confusion
But I know it's the devil trying to block my view.
He creates the thunder to steal my joy
But I am following God on what to do.

You see, when you follow God
It doesn't matter what type of storm comes through,
Because I am stepping out on faith
So the God can guide me.

Changes Through Life
(Middle School Life)

October 30, 1994

As I look back to last year,
1994 was a rough year,
Which words can only show.

First it was gossiping,
Having a hurtful tongue like a snake toward people,
Although I have stopped all of that.
Now it's gone to another situation.

I'm starting to smart off at teachers.
In fact, I had to sit by myself for a week.
I had silent lunch for three days.
What new things will I seek?

I gave answers to a test,
Which I know I was wrong in doing,
But cousins stick together
Like brother, like sister.

I brought a Gameboy to school,
I got it taken away,
I got it back through hard work;
I call it nothing but bad luck.

One important lesson it taught me
Was always tell the truth,
'Cause if you dodge the problem
It will haunt you like a ghost until you do.

The first time is always easy,
The second time might not be.
But the main thing I was wondering:
Why does the bad choices always happen to me?

I still don't know the answer to the question
But I'm learning something new day by day,
And by the time I learn the real reason
I will make a promise
To myself and anyone who reads this:
I am going to give everything my all
Because I have the potential for greatness.

Surviving the Storm

As we travel down the path of life God has given us,
We often reflect on the good and the bad.
Our memories remind us of the sun as the rain turns into a rainbow.
While other reflections are like a storm that makes us sad.

I hear claps of thunder
And then lightning strikes that causes pain
But God comes by with his angels
To bring me happiness and bring you praise.

The road we travel on is dark and gloomy with clouds,
But as long as you let God be your leader,
He will guide you to a path to make you proud.

The road we travel on is clear with the sun shining bright outside.
As people, we sometimes think about and wonder if a person has lied.

When God is standing by your side
Like a soldier protecting the battlefield,
He will always shine down from heaven
To provide a special shield.

Experiencing a Breakthrough

My God is my Provider and my strength through many trials and tribulations,
like a windstorm coming through,
he blocks the twisters and tornadoes that destroy various things.

He is the Almighty, the Omniscient,
Who has the power to do what he wants to do.
When I jump over hurdles
I shout, "In Jesus' name."

When the breakthrough happens
I lift my arms up to praise his name,
Because without his presence,
I would find fault and have everyone to blame.

I see in my dream a breakthrough is coming
With a shower of blessings.
My blessings might be financial or emotional,
And only God can give me my breakthrough.

I Wish I Would Have Listened

It was a week before it happened
That my mother told me to cut down that tall, half-dead tree.
I had no idea when I disobeyed
The consequences that God wanted me to see.

I was hard-headed and stubborn
But then I started seeing those weather warnings from WSB-TV.
I will never forget that month of April;
The year was 2016.

The news started flashing these storm warnings
While my eyes followed the path of the weather map on TV.
At first the storm hit Coweta, then Meriwether, Heard, and Troup,
It said the town of Hogansville,
So my eyes followed the path of watching the news,
Like a hawk to stay in the loop.

At first I heard a clap and it was thunder;
Then I saw a light flash before my eyes.
The skies had turned darker.
In the back of my head, I had to say, "Oh, my. This storm is really coming"

The meteorologist on the news
Stated the storm was coming through.
He stated the city, street, and time,
And they warned everyone that it was time for them to take cover.

The wind started howling like a coyote
And the lights went dark inside the house.
I heard a loud boom and then the house shook.
And things were as so silent one could hear a pin drop.

Suddenly, I felt water come inside the house
Because the window broke.
The lightning struck the top of the tree,
Causing it to break in several pieces and hit the house.

Some people don't realize how strong and powerful the wind is,
Even my car endured damage.
Lightning continued to flash
As the rain poured into a flood.

I dropped down to my knees to ask God,
"What message did you want me to focus on?"
God wanted me to slow down and follow the correct path,
Because with his love and guidance
I could conquer the grapes of wrath.

God wanted me to change my way of thinking
And have an understanding heart,
Always find forgiveness.
So I could find the right way to start.

Church

We should all go to church,
Whether the sun is shining outside or if we see the moon's reflection
We learn about God and how to be faithful in many ways.

One way we learn about God is from the Holy Bible;
The other way is from the message the preacher has to say.
Church is a place to come to each Sunday morning
To learn the wonderful things about God
So you can change your direction of life

Without God and church
Life would not be nothing.
You should get down on your knees to pray for people and their different situations daily.

Don't go to church just to be going;
Always go to church
To learn a lifelong lesson about God.

Section 3:
Relationships

If I Could See You Face to Face

If I could see you face to face
I would have so many things to say,
But since I don't know when that will be,
I am going to send you a message my own special way.

We've been talking for several months
Through social media, text, and telephone,
But through it all
It doesn't seem like we have ever left each other alone.

I realize I leave you in a state of confusion
Because you really never know where my head will be.
Some answers are very simple, where I'm completely honest
And other times are more complicated because I don't tell you everything.

If I could see you face to face
A lot of questions could be answered.
One day you asked me the question,
"What do you want from me?"

I apologized that I should have said this verbally, but again, I'd rather talk to you face to face
I want you to be my "lover" for a lifetime,
But there are some experiences I want to have along the way.
I bet you are wondering what I'm talking about,
So let me explain what I'm trying to say.

Do you remember when I talked about dating, being engaged, and being married?
Well, there's a reason I said what I did.
That all could take place in around six months
If that's truly the Lord's will.

I want to spend time with you,
Cuddling and holding hands.
I want the world to know that we are a couple,
And that we can together rule the land.

I want the experience of getting a ring and you getting down on one knee,
We look into each other's eyes,
And you ask the question
"Will you marry me?"

I want to experience all of the bridal showers
That would come from family and friends.
After all, we are both in the same profession,
(And in our profession people can give some of the best wedding gifts.)

I want the experience of picking out and gathering up my bridesmaids,
And showing everyone how we confess our love for each other.
My brother or dad gives me away.

Weddings can be expensive,
But not if we strategically plan.
I want to walk down the aisle of a church
In the center with us holding hands.

With both of us having the same career
And living on the opposite side of the state,
This is the stuff that we need to start planning now
Instead of several months later.

I know you don't like premarital counseling,
But it's something to really think through.
In the state of Georgia it saves you money
For the marriage certificate, and it is more dollars than just a few.

I know this makes your head spin,
But this is how I best express myself
As I type this freestyle.
I want to be committed to you,
And stand by your side.

I want to be right with you;
I will definitely not try to hide.
I want you to talk to me
When something is bothering you.
I want to help any pain go away
And show you a variety ways that I love you.

Thinking I'm in Love

My heart beats uncontrollably
Not because I'm alive;
Because I have fallen in love.
But a lot of these feelings I've tried to hide.

I reconnected with this guy from long ago
Through social media back in July,
But before that I put his name in Google
And found out that he went from teaching middle to high.

I talk to him in the early hours of each morning
About everything from A to Z.
I have a hard time hanging up the phone from him
Because of the conversations he has with me.

We are not in a serious relationship,
But why do I feel like we are?
The time that we had spent with each other,
I could see the moon, the sun, and stars shining brighter than I did before..

I have tried to turn my feelings off,
But feelings are not something that you can turn off or on.
For some reason I feel closer and closer and with just me and him,
I want our time alone.

I want to show him I love him,
To show him how much I care.
I want the pain and stress that he's feeling
To vanish.

I know that I'm crazy in saying this
But I think I'm about to lose my mind.
This guy lives at a distance
So the biggest thing that keeps me from him is distance and time.

Several years have gone by quickly
But honestly it doesn't seems that long ago.
That was actually the last time I had originally spoken to him.
But why does it seem like yesterday?

Both of us are much older now
And better at managing our lives.
But why did we start back talking to each other now
If it wasn't meant to be?

My mind is telling me different things,
But my body is telling me yes.
My heart belongs to him
And I need to let my soul confess.

I think about this guy all the time;
My mind is on him 24/7.
I'm even staring at the phone,
Wondering if he will or will not answer.

So, God, what is wrong with me?
Have I truly fallen in love?
He is the only person I want to be with
And allow my family to know.

Will things truly work out for us this time?
That's something that only God knows,
But this go-round my love is stronger,
And it will be harder to let things go.

It's Worth the Wait!

My life is trapped in a bubble
And it seems like I have no place to go.
People have turned their backs to me;
My friends, family, and lovers have stooped to a new low.

It seems like the people I turn to for help
Will not give me the time of day,
But in turn when they need help
I'm standing with them along the way.

I realize that I am no angel
And I have done things in my life to have a wicked past,
But in this journey called life,
I know that trouble will not always last.

I once told a friend of mine,
You must let that anger and bitterness go,
Because holding on to the devil's path
Will not allow a person to grow.

Sometimes we are faced with situations in your life
And we don't always get what we want.
Do you break it off completely?
Or hold on to faith and not lose hope?

I drop down on my knees to pray
And ask God, "Why does everything seem to be going wrong?"
He answers me by saying, "You've been through hell and high water to make you strong."
But you have to follow God's path in order to receive the key to his kingdom.

God replies by saying, "Life will throw you many obstacles and curveballs."
It leaves you clueless about what to do.
Sometimes we want things
And it's not our time to get them,
But if God wants you to have them
You can claim and speak them into existence.

Never lose hope about things in life,
No matter how bad things may look.
Keep God first in everything you do
And it will change the initial path you took.

Patience is a virtue,
Which is something most people don't have,
But something that is meaningful is worth the wait
And eventually will come to pass.

As My Dreams Come True
May 15, 1995

Love has hit the air like Cupid flying through the sky
With my dream that comes true.
Today is that special day
That I share only with you.

Over the years that I have spent
Looking up toward the sky,
I look to the Lord and ask him,
Should I have been searching even so high?

As I look into the beginning,
I see our future ahead.
I have a vision that comes from within us
And the love your heart has led.

At first I didn't realize
What the word "love" really meant,
Until my dream of this day came true.

Now it's about to happen,
As we take each other's vows.
We're finally going to be together,
For better, for worse,
For richer, for poorer,
Till death do us part.

We shall always be together
With every beat of my heart.

True Love

I love you,
And I'm saying this from the heart.
When I first laid eyes on you
I loved you from the start.

A first I didn't realize
How lovely and fine you looked,
But now that we have a relationship,
I guarantee I won't mess it up.

Now that you're my baby
I'm as happy as can be.
This is the best time in my life
And it's going down in history.

One time before I go
I have to say it again:
"I love you, I love you, I love you,
And I hope this never ends."

May My Dream Come True

As I lay my head on my pillow
I close my eyes to dream,
A dream that predicts my future in five to ten years
And the trials and tribulations I may face.

I fast-forward to the next year to see a book.
This book is small and paperback with many pages;
It just received publication in bookstores around the world.

I fast-forward to mid-year
And I see writing as a career,
A talent that God gave to me took a break for several years
But God whispered in my ear,
"You have to make a move."

I see a house and a car in my dream.
I know if I have faith, it will come to pass,
But only if I believe.

My dream pictures me sitting at a desk taking an exam
With a lot of studying and praying.
The exam results are exactly my answered prayers.
My exam was a book that was written
And published for all to see

My obedience in Jesus causes me to be nationally known
Because I have a special message from heaven to spread
That comes from the Lord up above.

I am proud of my special talent to feel the presence from the Lord,
And with his help
His message is carried from the heart.

How It Should Have Been

Sometimes in life we want things we can't have.
Is it time to give up or time to wait?
It's always great to tell the truth and not tell any lies,
But what you do in the dark
Will eventually come to light, so there is no need to hide.

Why get close to someone
When you know it's not going to go anywhere in the long run?
Never start something that you can't finish,
Because it gives the other person false hope.

Sometimes it's important to talk so you can hear what the other person wants,
Especially if you are going to form a relationship, so you'll know the dos and don'ts.

If you are involved in a relationship already
You need to leave the person who you are talking to on the phone alone.
You need to leave the other person alone.
A friend is a friend, even if it's from a distance.
You either love the person who you talk on the phone with
And be willing to make future plans
Or move on with the person whom you are currently in a relationship with.
Even if you might be trapped in a bubble.

If you were in love with someone six months ago,
Explain to me how quickly things have changed.
How can your heart be in another place?
Where exactly was it at in the beginning?

Although we may be soulmates
You never have gave our relationship a chance
God will put us together if it's meant to be
And nothing will be able to split us apart,
Even if it's destiny.

What Is a Dad?

(Dedicated to my brother Bennie Rhodes, Jr.)

My dad is a leader
Who is in charge of the household.
He gives the instructions and rules
And tells me what I need to be told.

My dad is a disciplinarian
Who punishes me when I do wrong,
And depending on what I do,
The punishment may be long.

My dad is a true Christian
Who reads his Bible every day.
He has a gift to help people
And help them make it along the way.

My dad is a father
Who truly encourages me with my future plans,
And he is one who helped me develop into the person that I am.

For the Father I Never Had

As I close my eyes,
I rewind the time to when I was fourteen years old.
I have a lot of confusion running through my mind about life in general,
Trying to keep my life on hold.

God sat beside me
And began to whisper in my ear,
"The advice that I will give you is solid and it will guide you to make the best decisions,
And be a person as strong as a lion, if you may."

As a teenager, I have had to watch myself grow into a young lady,
Trying to learn not to be persuaded by television ads on drugs and sex in this dangerous world on my own.
My biggest wish as a child is having two loving parents
Who would get up at the crack of dawn to cook me breakfast.
I close my eyes to make a wish.

My wish is to have a relationship with my father,
To have a person I call my dad.
So I could have a man to talk to
About the good times in my life and about anytime things got bad as a storm with the thunder and lightning
Passing through the night.
I have seen so many fathers and daughters together that it makes me wish that I could be with mine.
Is that a difficult request to make?

I would often cry myself to sleep,
Still wishing that things could change in the blink of an eye.
A message I would like to say to any father:
"Children are a special thing
that you should always give your time and love in return."

Dear Mama

Dear Mama,
You are the only parent that has been there through thick and thin.
I know that I am a hard-headed child,
But you have always showed me love, respect, and care.
To my mother that I have,
I'm blessed that you're alive.
I shall be that daughter
You always wanted,
To give you safety, protection, and strength,
And that strong, careful pride.

If Only You Were Here

"Only if you were here"
Is a phrase often said.
I'm only a teenage girl
Reaching out for my only dad.

I'm going through my teenage life,
And what a hormonal time it is to face.
One day he will regret it,
But then it will be too late.

I have finally realized there is no hope,
I'll continue to sob these lonely tears.
But none of this would have ever have happened
Only if you were here.

Section 4:
Holidays and Months

January

The howling wind begins to blow outside
And the temperature drops to freezing cold.
And the weatherman says that the precipitation freezes like ice to the ground
It feels like a popsicle outside.

So people know the bad weather is about to come.
Some people gather at the grocery store while some people are reading the Book of Psalms.
The sleet turns into snow overnight
While the temperature continues to drop.

The roadway is filled with black ice
And the DOT is trying to fill the roadway with salt.
The children in the mountains
Are excited to have some days off from school.

During the mysterious weather season
God can make an entire city stop.
He has a message to give in order for people to listen.
Sometimes the weather takes a turn for the worse
For people to understand the true meaning.

Always listen to God with the message that he sends through the Holy Spirit.
The wind, the rain, the thunder, the lightning,
Are all symbolic of a message God is sending everyone across the world:
Be peaceful to your fellow neighbor so we can join together
Instead of falling apart He wants us to have the peace, joy, and happiness, and not the fire from the pits of hell.

February

February is second month that symbolizes love
And it represents love, hearts, teddy bears, and candy-what one can only want.
Relationships around the world
Are celebrated in many different ways;
From eating dinner to watching a movie,
Couples honor their special day.

Love is about two people who care for one another.
It's about spending time with the one you love,
And making them feel special and romantic
And showing them love and affection.

He Bore the Cross for Me

We gather here to honor
Another joyous day,
For this one is the most special,
But what are we celebrating?

We are celebrating Easter today
To remember the man who bore the cross.
He died for the love of everyone,
But then one day he arose.

When he arose it showed
That he will always be our friend;
Through sin, joys, and sorrows,
He shall stick there until the end.

Jesus will not put on you
Any more than you can bear,
'Cause if Jesus can bear the cross,
You can in turn be born again.

This was Jesus Christ
Showing the nation who he loved, for there is no hate in his body,
Showing we can all rise above sin.

We must look to the Lord and thank him
For what he has done for us.
Jesus, keep me near the cross,
'Cause he bore the cross for me.

To My Mother, With Love

As a special day that comes
Only once a year,
One word, "mother,"
Is what we want to hear.

The second Sunday in May
Has come once again
To observe a celebration
For mothers around the world.

What do I think of when it comes to Mother's Day?
I think of all the things
That have happened along the way.

I think of all the love
That a mother can give a child.
Every time I think of my mother,
To my face comes a smile.
I think of all the good times
And the happiness that you have brought,
The loving, caring, and faithfulness,
And the lessons that you have taught.

There is one special message
That I would like to say,
And that is the phrase "I love you, mom"
And "Happy Mother's Day."

What Is a Mother?

What is a mother?
A mother is love.
She is the one who receives guidance from the Lord up above.

She is the wisdom and the light
To help you overcome the ultimate challenges in life.

My mother is the encouragement for you to do your best,
Like my teacher once told me,
Through my mother's guide
You will shine above the rest.

She is the spiritual leader
Who is guided by the way of faith
And teaches her children to love the ones whom they hate.

She is also a person who stands up for her rights;
Similar to the book of Corinthians,
She walks by faith and not by sight.

A mother is a guide
That can help you along the way,
So you can become grateful
And come back to thank her one day.

What is a mother?
I was asked, and I said,
"She is my best friend that will be there until the end".

My Mother's Love

A baby was born in September.
A mother was blessed with a baby girl.
After having this girl named Ann,
Everything changed in the entire world.

She already had two sons,
One named Bennie, Jr., and one son named Roy Lee.
In the young lives of all her children,
She didn't know how things would be.

She loves her children dearly,
Having jobs working odds and ends.
Jesus Christ steps in and helps us,
Because truly the love from the mother's heart
Is where it all begins.

Bennie, Jr., graduated Salutatorian
In the class of '85;
Roy Lee is still out there,
With himself he's trying to find.

Ann is only going to the tenth grade
While she looks to the Lord up above,
But the most special gift she's ever received
Is the gift of her mother's love.

Section 5:
School Thoughts

It Was Here Today, But Gone Tomorrow

When I close my eyes and think back to yesterday,
I visualize many years ago.
I dream about a memory
That everyone in Hogansville should know.

I reflect back to fall of 1994.
Tragedy happened.
That made our school community start over.

Hollering sirens, red lights, and fire trucks
Awoke the community, and some people could do all but speak.

People experienced many emotions,
Such as joy, fear, and shock.
(Students were able to miss some days from school.)
Our community came together and cooperated to help out during this tragic time.

"How can we make it better in this community today?
This electrical fire happened over the weekend,
And with the help of our community,
We will come back stronger putting back together all of the pieces.
There are so many problems but there's got to be a way."

Although it has been months
Since our school went away,
Our memories of our school are still strong
And we wish that it was here today.

I remember all of the good times we had in school,
But now there is a lot of emptiness and a lot of pain.
We must look to the Lord and thank him
And praise him for his name for the memories that he has brought us.
Shall we always remain the same?

It has been several months
Since it left us here all alone,
Since we heard the fireman say,
"So sorry, your school is gone!"

School Days

As the Earth revolves around the Sun
And the days go on and on,
I feel as happy and relaxed as if I were lying down on the couch,
But as our path throughout school continues,
It's important to know the facts.

One must look up to the heavens to ask,
"Am I satisfied with myself?
In every way humanly possible,
Do I make the best decisions?
Without thinking about it, or do I give a minute's delay?"

I am good to tell secrets to;
I always have a listening ear.
If I have an urge to speak
I can shout it all with a pen.

I have a love of going to school,
And everyone should know
I want to gain more wisdom and knowledge
So I can go through life obeying God's law.

Life Choices

Gossip is a hobby, like collecting baseball cards.
Spreading rumors is a choice to make sure you are heard.
Lying is an alternative to make sure that you have the last word.

An argument contains a lot of hatred
And violence is like a war.
Citizens are using guns illegally
With children who are caught in the core.

All of the children are joining gangs
Because they are not receiving any love.
Love is being received in the wrong places
Instead of praying on their hands and knees to the Lord up above.

Drugs have taken over the world
Like a wildfire spreading smoke.
It can destroy the whole entire village like a bulldozer,
Preventing any human from being able to cope.

In order to gain the key to success,
He or she must open their eyes wide
And lean on the Lord above
For him to be their spiritual guide.

Testing Prayer

Dear Lord,
I begin to close my eyes
As I drop down on my knees to pray.
I ask God for a shower of protection and knowledge
As Georgia schools begin their testing days.

I pray that you give the teachers patience
As students log in on their computers to take the test.
I pray that the Wi-Fi has a strong signal and the test has no glitches
So the students can do their best.

I pray that the teachers are protected from any sickness,
Which includes the flu and the cold.
I hope that the teachers drink plenty of liquid, like caffeine,
To read those test directions over and over.

I pray that the teacher's classrooms are test-ready
And the students are seated in rows.
I hope the students used what they have learned this year
To show their student growth.

I pray that teachers remember the rules:
That these tests travel everywhere they go,
From the bathroom to the workroom,
or stay secured in the classroom.

I pray these students use their knowledge
When they type their extended and constructed response.
I hope they use their scratch paper
To write down their thoughts and begin a draft.

I pray the students read the passages carefully.
In fact, I hope they read them more than once.

I pray for the testing coordinators
Who had to complete the trainings and get the testing materials prepared.
I hope that each testing day runs smoothly
Without any testing irregularities.

My biggest prayer is that students don't stress over the GMAs
And don't worry whether it's pass or fail.
It's important that we give that mindset,
That if we believe, we will excel.

Graduation Wisdom

I'm your guardian angel from heaven
Who has a special message.
I am a bird now who is spreading my wings
To remind you all of my love.

I know the road you've traveled on
Has been a rough like sandpaper feels,
But in the upcoming weeks and months
You will leave the cocoon and become a butterfly,
Because this graduation is here.

Remember all of the things I've taught you,
On how to survive, as you enter this world,
I have the faith like a grain of a mustard seed
Because you can make any dream come true.

As you keep your hopes and dreams alive
My spirit is with you like a tiger that gives you strength
To have a future that's completely brighter.

School Changes

The school year is finally coming to a close,
With Hogansville High School closing its doors,
But there's a history around it all,
From big, short, small, and tall students.

If you want to hear this story,
Let's begin.
If you want to add anything,
Just jump right in.

It all started in third grade.
Yes, back then we had it made.
I loved school without a doubt,
Way back when we could scream and shout.

Class of 1999 had it rough.
Look at things now; they are even more tough.
We would try to move up in every kind of way
But things would change day by day.

We went from one school; the middle school
And we had to say another year.
The middle school was on the same campus as the high school
So just about all of us
Could shed a tear.

Happy Birthday, Mr. Wearden!

Happy birthday to a teacher
Who taught me a year ago.
On this day you have gotten older
And your age, nobody knows!

Still thinking about the things you said,
I am living up to my full potential
And have changed my malicious way.
All the gossip I used to do
Is left back in the olden days.

I am serious and straightforward
And honest as can be.
I figure since I am in high school,
Being successful is the key.

Jaime Smith

I know a person who's short,
And she plays the saxophone.
When Hogansville School System consolidates with Troup County School System
She will be long gone.

She'll be missed by many people,
One of those people will be me.
This reason is because
We won the section of the week in band class with our instrument,.

We got mad at each other.
It was late in the year.
She's the best saxophone partner I've had.
We always would work together
On the newspaper staff.

We have a lot of memorable moments
That make us just sit back and laugh.
I'll really truly miss her
In that saxophone section.
She was my buddy, my pal, and I love her like a sister.

Mrs. Williams

Nice, sweet, and kind
Is a person that I know,
Full of charge and admiration
That words can only show.

Going throughout the hallway,
She plants a smile on every face with
Encouraging words for everyone
To take upon each day.

We are glad to have her,
Hope she stays for many more years to come.
She's a teacher whom we can trust
And know we always love.

Mrs. Pflueger

A person who can be sweet as a pie.
I bet in her spare time
She likes to get plenty of rest and sleep.

I haven't known her for a very long time;
It has only been a year.
Even though I never had her as a teacher,
She is as precious as a rose and always so sincere.

We don't have that many things in common
But I really like her style.
She enjoys taking her long walks,
Because she walks several miles.

I admire Mrs. Pflueger
Like the sun that's bright outside.
She's a great teacher who helps students
Look ahead and reach for the stars.

Bennie Rhodes, Jr.
(My Brother)

He is my brother,
Sweet as he can be.
He buys different things,
For his little sister, you see.

He'll go out of his way
To do things for me.
He is more than just a brother;
He is like a father, as you can see.

We get along well,
He takes me every place he goes.
If we don't agree on something
We'll make a decision to and fro.

He's fun to be around,
He's fun to talk to,
He has his own house,
And I have to say, I love you, big bro.

Mrs. Spradlin

Mrs. Spradlin was my math teacher,
Sweet as she can be.
In the years she has been a teacher
She is put down in history.

I like her as a teacher,
I like her as a friend.
I hope that even though she's leaving
This bond will never end.

She is an enthusiastic motivating teacher,
Which everyone should know.
I hope as the years go by and by
She will always be a pro.

To Dena Spradlin, the funny one,
We shall miss you day by day.
I hope you enjoy where you're going
And come back and visit along the way.

A Teacher and Teaching

When a teacher wakes up in the morning
He has students on his mind.
The creative wheels of the brain are turning
To ensure that all students are learning and don't fall behind.

You see, teachers have dreams in their sleep
Of how to keep their students engaged.
It may be hands-on with manipulatives,
Or hand motions through song or highlighting text on a page.

Teaching involves all kinds of paperwork
From parent conferences, phone, IEP meetings, and testing.
When testing happens in the spring,
Teachers have to cover up bulletin boards to prevent a testing violation.

Teachers even have to take work home,
Whether it's to plan or grade papers.
Teaching is not a nine-to-five job;
Teachers work morning, afternoons, nights, and evenings.

Teaching is an actual calling.
That God has inspired you to do,
Because with all of the hurdles and challenges of education,
Without God you can't make it through.

What Is a Teacher?

"What is a teacher?"
I was asked one day.
I knew what it was,
But what could I say?

A teacher is a parent
Who provides when he or she is away from home.
We provide food, clothing, and supplies,
So the real parent is never alone.

A teacher is a doctor,
Because sometimes we have to give medical aid.
We store Vaseline and Band-Aids
To help make it through the day.

A teacher is a lawyer,
Because sometimes students will argue and fight each other.
The teacher is even a detective,
Before switching to their administrator.

A teacher is a rock star,
Because we are told to keep our lessons engaging.
With hands-on manipulatives and a variety of songs,
Every lesson taught is amazing.

"What is a teacher?"
I was asked one day.
It is a calling, I answered, from God
To be a positive figure and change a child's life along the way.

Section 6:
Other Poems

Where I Go, Someone's There

Wherever I go
It's someone there.
No matter where I am
It follows me everywhere.

I can't use the bathroom,
I can't sleep at night,
Whatever I try to do
It's always there to fight.

I can't deal with it at school,
I can't deal with it at home.
Sometime the phone rings right beside me.

I try to talk about it;
It doesn't solve it one bit.
I guess it's one of those things
That I'll have to live with.

I've got to stop this now;
I can't take it anymore.
I guess I'll try to punch or shoot the door.

It's a shame when it ends especially if you can't see
The things that you do that are really hurting me.

I wish that you would stop
Because I can see where you may be,
And realize all of the hurt
Before you try to flee.

Wherever I may go,
I know I'm still being followed
with the times of the ungratefulness
And all of the times of despair.

It Was Just a Test

Some things in life happen for a reason
While some journeys are made up of a test.
It's not a game where you win or lose;
It's simply how you handle the situation or circumstance.

The wind starts howling strongly
As the trees start leaning back and forth.
Your mind wanders off about those decisions
To think about all it's worth.

God teaches various lessons
To see which path we choose to go.
Because sometimes the path we decide to follow
Leads us to more than what we really know.

We are all God's athletes
Who run the race that he said we should follow,
But before we cross the finish line,
Things happen that are hard for us to swallow.

Sometimes God prepares us for this test
By giving us notes and hints along the way,
But some people will fail this extensive exam
And some people will excel because they listened to what God had to say.

When God sends his angels down
With a special message for you to hear,
He is only preparing you for the test
Because he wants you to continue in life
Without any fear.

Stand by Me

I want you to stand by me
So I will not have to be alone.
I need your love and support
Because you help me when I'm right and wrong.

I need for you to be with me
To take care of me when I'm sick
I need you
To be with me and not nitpick.

I need you to stand by my side
And believe in me every step of the way,
And regardless of how things turn out,
I know that you will stay.

I need for you to stand by me
With their belief in God, too,
Because in this journey called life,
It's the only way to see it through.

What Is a Family?

"What is family?",
I was asked one day.
I wanted to describe mine to you
So I had a lot of things to say.

A family has siblings that you sit down to talk with;
They can give you advice
Regardless if you really want to hear it.

A family has a mother or father that can guide you on your life's path
And help you figure out those lifelong expectations and how to budget your money with math.

You can ask them about future mates
And they will tell you how they feel,
But don't get upset by what they say
Because the parents are just keeping it real.

A family cares for one another
And will stick by each other through thick and thin.
Even when things are complicated,
They will help you repent of your sin.

"What is a family?",
I was asked one day.
It is sticking by each other's sides
And being faithful with loyalty.

Work Hard for Your Blessings
(Dedicated to the mother who had her children taken away.)

The road that you travel on may seem difficult
As it sometimes will.
Stay strong because you are a fighter
And over time God will heal the wounds that you have encountered.

God has you here for a reason,
Your biggest blessings are two and five.
For those two blessings there is hope to push harder and stay alive.

Regardless of how dark this journey may get
And what obstacles you have to face,
I want you to pray and ask God,
"Will you help me fight to win this race?"

When you make it to the finish line
With a couple of hiccups along the way,
You will say it was a job well done,
I'm so glad I stayed
and God helped to protect my children and me along the way.

Faith Is my Belief

Times can get rough,
But as you see God reach the sky,
She gives you a shield of protection
Wherever your trouble may lie.

This shield will protect you
From Satan and the fire that is straight ahead,
But as a preacher truly says,
From James 2:20,
"Faith without work is dead."

Everywhere you go,
Your angel will be your shining light.
You may think the light looks dim
But instead it's actually bright.

The road seems very rocky
From the journey I travel on each day,
But I will hold the hands of God
So I can make it along the way.

God will guide me on the path
That should be the straight and narrow just ahead.
As long as I lean on God,
I know that I will be spiritually fed.

I will keep moving forward with God
Regardless of the curves and hills I pass,
Because I know with the help of God
Trouble will not always last.

My Gift

My spirit has left me
But my body is still here on earth.
My soul is going to the gates of heaven,
But how will people remember me?
How much was my life worth?

When the Lord whispered softly
To tell me he was about to call my name,
I had tears of joy and mixed emotions,
But I questioned myself,
"Am I the one I need to blame for leaving this earth so soon?"

You see, many people on this earth
Has a special talent or a gift
That you must go through the journey of life to complete.

You may steer away from it,
But it's the puzzle pieces put together
To give you the special lift.

Once your journey in life is complete
And you have used your special gift,
God will say, "Well done, my good and faithful servant!"
For a life that has been well-lived.
Thank you for caring about my message
In the way I wanted you to;
I'm glad that you followed direction and guidance for the path that seemed hopeless.

The Saxophone

I played the alto saxophone in middle school.
I played it for three years.
The saxophone makes clear, sharp sounds
Which we all can hear.

As a musician, you must have a neck strap for this instrument.
If you don't want to buy a saxophone
You may rent instead.

Reading music is not always easy,
But sometimes it can be fun.
When you try out for band,
One must practice, practice, practice,
Because it takes a lot of work to get it done.

You have to have a reed
In order to play the alto sax.
Sit back and listen to the music
That is very soothing that can make him relax.

When one plays musical notes,
Those musical notes can very high.
Sometimes you can meditate when they hear the music to help you answer the question why.

What Is Being Faithful?

"What is being faithful?"
I was asked one day.
It is being loyal and steadfast
To any person along the way.

If a person is faithful,
They are honest to all the parties involved.
They answer all of the questions
No matter how much it may hurt the ego.

How can you talk a certain way to another significant other all the time,
But the other significant other is the one whose spending time with your family.
And you have someone else on your mind?

If you know that you are unhappy,
Move on to what you want to do,
But when God makes his final call,
He is not going to ask for anyone else, only you.

You can't go around life
Making other people happy.
Think about yourself first,
Because if you don't take care of yourself,
Following what other people do can make your life worse.

"What is being faithful?",
I was asked one day.
It is telling the truth to all the parties involved,
Even if you have committed the ultimate sin.
It's better to come clean instead of someone finding out over time.

About the Author

ANN RHODES is the author of *From the Beginning Until Now,* her first book of poetry, which went into publication in 2016. When she was an elementary school student, God blessed her with a talent that she didn't discover until she was in sixth grade, during her middle-school years. Over the time span of several years, a variety of her poems have been published in the *Hogansville Herald, LaGrange Daily News,* and even WSB-TV in a "Please, Stop the Violence" campaign. Three poems, "A Great Man," "The Greatest Easter Gift," and "What Is a Mother?" have been published in different poetry anthologies throughout the United States. The poem "A Great Man" is a part of a CD collection incorporated by Poetry.com. She is currently an elementary-school teacher with a bachelor's, a master's, and a specialist degree from Troy University. She enjoys writing poetry and spreading God's message to people all over the world.

www.ingramcontent.com/pod-product-compliance
Lightning Source LLC
Chambersburg PA
CBHW050041080526
44586CB00014B/1403